The
Ross Hannas:
Living, Laughing, Loving

WAYNE GRINSTEAD

Illustrated by John Ham

BROADMAN PRESS
Nashville, Tennessee

© Copyright 1986 • Broadman Press
All rights reserved
4243-25
ISBN: 0-8054-4325-8
Dewey Decimal Classification: J266.092
Subject Headings: HANNA, ROSS // HANNA, BETTY JANE // MISSIONS—ARIZONA
Library of Congress Catalog Card Number: 86-6807

Library of Congress Cataloging-in-Publication Data

Grinstead, Wayne, 1946-
  The Ross Hannas : living, laughing, loving.

  (Meet the missionary series)
  Summary: Discusses the lives and work of Ross and
Betty Jane Hanna, home missionaries in Arizona.
  1. Hanna, Ross—Juvenile literature. 2. Hanna,
Betty Jane—Juvenile literature. 3. Indians of North
America—Southwest, New—Missions—Juvenile literature.
4. Missionaries—Southwest, New—Biography—Juvenile
literature. [1. Hanna, Ross. 2. Hanna, Betty Jane.
3. Missionaries] I. Ham, John, ill. II. Title.
III. Series.
E78.S7H254 1986   266'.6132'0922 [B] [920] 86-6807
ISBN 0-8054-4325-8

To Ross and Betty Jane's children and grandchildren
and all other children and young people who read this book.
May you become inspired, as I was, by the lives and works
of
Ross and Betty Jane Hanna.

Contents

Foxes and Hounds

It was July 23, 1939. I was eleven years old. My older brother
and his kids were visiting. We were playing fox and hounds. I
was the fox.

The warm July sun cast long shadows across the field of
Kentucky bluegrass. Suddenly, a boy burst from the forest
and ran full speed into the meadow. Close behind were six
more children, pulling forest thorns and vines from their
hair and clothing as they ran.

The eleven-year-old boy reached the other side of the
meadow and ran into the forest. He threw his arms in front
of his face to knock away the forest brush. The thorns
snagged his hair and scratched the sides of his face, but he
kept running. "The hounds," he told himself, "were close
and gaining. I can't slow down." To slow down was to be
caught. To be caught was to lose the game.

The boy dodged large trees, jumped over small shrubs,
and climbed under a barbed-wire fence. The pack of six
closed in, yelping and barking like dogs.

"They're too close," he thought. "Gotta do something
quick."

He spied a tall yellow poplar tree on the edge of a small
clearing. With his last bit of energy he sprinted to the tree,
grabbed its trunk in a bear hug, and shinned up to the first
large limb, twenty feet up.

"You'll never make it," Ross Hanna yelled from the top
of the tree. "I'm safe, and I won. The fox has beaten the
hounds once again."

Two of the hounds tried to climb the tree as Ross had
done seconds before. But the two, Ross's cousins who were

visiting, could not climb trees without limbs. After several unsuccessful and painful tries they gave up.

"All right, Ross," yelled the oldest boy, "you won this one. Come on down, and let's get home for dinner."

"You're sure?" Ross yelled back. "You won't try to catch me when I get down?"

"I promise," the boy yelled back. "If I do, you can have all my corn bread at supper tonight." When Ross heard that he almost hoped the children would chase him again, if that's what it took to get a double helping of corn bread.

Ross swung down and threw his legs around the tree trunk. His hands still held firmly to the limb. He pulled his right hand from the limb and hugged the trunk.

"Ross Hanna," said the youngest girl, "you look just like a monkey hanging . . ."

It happened so quickly she could not finish the sentence. The dry limb cracked like a rifle shot. Ross lunged backwards. The children screamed in terror as he fell headfirst toward the ground.

Halfway down Ross hit a small limb. The impact flipped him over and left a deep gash in his chin. But it probably saved his life. A second later Ross was on the ground, lying across a sprawling root at the base of the tree.

Ross knew he was badly hurt. His right leg, between the hip and the knee, was broken. The bone had broken through the skin and was sticking in the soft ground. The doctor would later call it a compound fracture. A cousin quickly ran the half mile home to get Ross's father.

Bad Times Are a Part of Life

A doctor cleaned and set my leg at home, but on the third day infection set in. We went to a hospital in Louisville, fifty miles away. They asked my father if they could amputate. He said, "No, save that boy's leg!"

Ross awoke and rubbed the sleep from his eyes. Beside his hospital bed stood his father, a tall man whose face was beginning to wrinkle from years of working out in the sun.

Price Hanna looked down at Ross. The boy's right leg was in traction and a metal pin held the bones together at the knee. Mr. Hanna wanted to stay at the hospital with Ross, but he could not. It was time to gather the crops, and that would not wait, not for an accident, not for anything. Ross had twelve brothers and sisters, six of them still living at home in Elizabethtown. They needed a father at home. Ross's father knew that, and so did Ross.

"I know you are busy on the farm," Ross said to his father. "You go back, I'll be all right here.

"I remember what you always taught me," Ross continued. "Bad times are a part of life; we must make the best of them and keep on going."

His father left, sad but proud.

I was in a four-bed ward for three months. The first month was pretty much a blank because my fever was so high. The second month I began to make progress.

From his bed in the corner of the children's ward, Ross looked out on an all-white world. The walls were white, the beds were white, the sheets were white, the doctor's coats were white; even the nurses' stockings and shoes were white.

It was the first time Ross had been inside a hospital. In fact, it was one of the few times he had been treated by a doctor. At the Hanna house, Ross's mother used a "doctor book." It always sat on the long bookshelf beside the family Bible. His mother had said that the Bible was the most important Book in the house. The doctor book was second.

"How are you doing this morning, Ross?" The nurse's words broke the boy's concentration. "You looked as if you were deep in thought," she continued.

"I was," he said. "I was thinking about home. How long have I been here? When do you think I can go home?"

The nurse leaned over and checked the chart on the end of the bed. "You came on July 26, and today is August 30. You've been here more than a month. As for when you can leave, well, that's up to the doctor."

Ross looked up at the nurse. She was young and pretty. She reminded him of his mother, except his mother's face was beginning to wrinkle just a little, and her hands were not as soft as the nurse's. "My mother's hands would be soft too," Ross said to himself, "if she didn't have to do farm work."

"What's that about your mother?" the nurse said.

"Was I talking out loud?" Ross asked. "I was just thinking about my mother," he continued. "She lives on our small farm outside of Elizabethtown."

"She and your father have been here to see you many times," the nurse said. "Don't you remember?"

"I sort of do," Ross replied. "But to tell the truth, I don't remember much that's happened since I've been here. Only the last day or so."

"Do you like living on a farm?" the nurse asked.

"I love it," said Ross. "I like to be busy, and there's always something to do on a farm. On Saturday afternoon and Sundays we play outside a lot. We have big trees in our front yard that go all the way down to the pond. We play

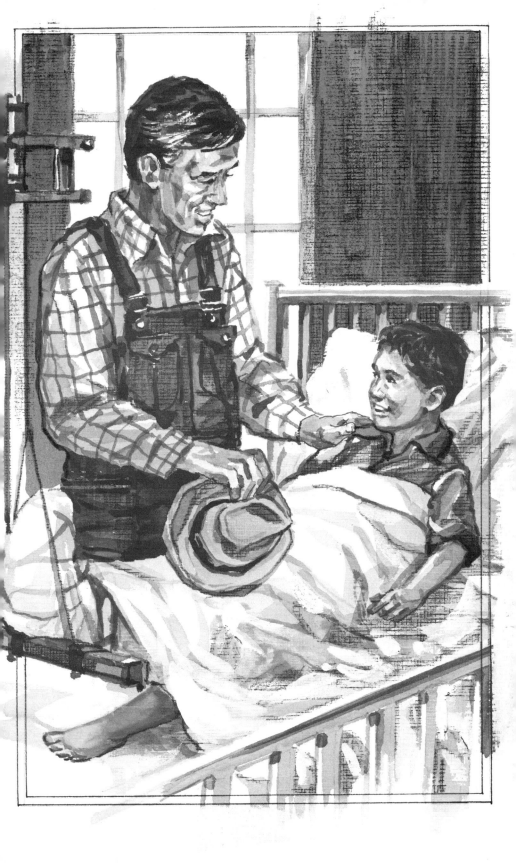

hide-and-seek there. Sometimes on Sundays we play church. And of course we all have chores."

"What kind of chores?" the nurse asked.

"You name it, and I do it," Ross replied. "I feed the chickens, pick tobacco, slop the hogs, and milk the cows. I even help my father separate the cream from the milk."

"What is your favorite chore?" the nurse asked, not really expecting a reply.

"I like to work out in the field with my father," said Ross. "He tells us tall tales as we work." Ross picked up a glass from the bedside table and took a sip of water through a clear glass straw. He had not talked so much in days, and his throat was dry.

The nurse put the glass back on the table. She noticed a large paper cup half filled with quarters, nickles, and dimes.

"What's this?" she asked.

"It's my goat cup," Ross replied.

"And what is a goat cup?" she said, trying to estimate the amount of money inside.

"I'm saving money to buy a goat when I get home. People who come to see me in the hospital have been bringing money instead of flowers. I'd rather have a goat than flowers," he said.

The nurse reached into her pocket. "I hope you get a very nice goat," she said, and dropped two quarters into the cup.

Home Again, Finally

The accident made life more serious. I remembered my father's words, "The success of a person is what they make of a bad situation." I accepted that, and was not bitter.

Ross came home after three months in the hospital. As his father drove the car up the winding dirt road to the house, Ross noticed that the maple trees in the front yard had shed their leaves. This was only natural, he told himself. After all, it was late October.

The wind was not blowing, but the cold quickly penetrated his light clothing. Once inside, Ross felt the warmth of the old drum stove in the front room taking away the chill. This large room was a family room and a bedroom for Ross's parents and several of his brothers and sisters. Ross spent the next six months there.

During the day Ross's mother taught him to sew, to crochet, to knit, and to hook rugs with old silk stockings. At least once a day Ross would sit at the window, admiring the two goats his father had bought for him. "I'd rather have a goat than flowers," he remembered telling the nurse at the hospital. He never imagined he would have two goats.

At night the family sat around the stove to keep warm, and Frances Hanna often read Bible stories. Ross was fascinated by what he heard. The story of Samson, the strong man, came alive in his imagination. As his mother read about the Tower of Babel, Ross could almost see it in his mind. Ross pictured the shepherd David and wondered how it would feel to battle a giant. In these Bible stories Ross found some important heroes.

By summer Ross was outside playing with his brothers

13

and sisters. His cast was off, but he could not bend his knee. The doctor had told him to expect that, especially since his knee had not been moved in almost a year.

Ross ran stiff legged when he played. He sat sideways in the pew at church. Sometimes his knee hurt. But no one remembers hearing him complain.

Getting Serious About Religion

We saved our gasoline so we could go to church on Sunday in the car. During the summer, when we didn't have gas money, we would ride in a wagon across several hills by way of a dirt road.

Ross could not remember the first time he went to church. He started going when he was so young, and he had gone so often. "Perhaps it was like eating," he thought. As hard as he tried, he could never remember his first meal.

The Hannas were members at Severns Valley Baptist Church. It was old and beautiful. There were exposed rafters in the ceilings and U-shaped pews that formed a semicircle around the pulpit. It was quite different from the play church that Ross often set up in the top of the hayloft.

"Where do you want me to sit?" asked Sue, Ross's younger sister.

"Right there," Ross responded, pointing his finger at a hay bale, "right by Neil."

"And who is the preacher today?" asked Neil.

"I will be the preacher today," Ross replied.

"But you were the preacher last Sunday," Neil reminded.

"That's because I made the game up, silly," Ross barked back. "When you make up a game for us to play, you can also make up the rules. And now, if you're through talking, we will begin."

The children reached forward for their pretend hymnbooks. Ross hummed a note, and away they went with "Amazing Grace." Playing church was fun for all the Hanna children, especially Ross. And the cows walking under the hayloft? They never seemed to mind at all.

After the pretend service, Ross often baptized some of his brothers and sisters. He even baptized some animals in the pond beyond the maple trees in front of their house. Old Jane, the family dog, seemed to enjoy the Sunday dunkings. The family cats, however, were not very cooperative.

Ross played church, but he was serious about religion, even before he became a Christian. Ross was fifteen years old before he actually accepted Christ. It happened during a revival at nearby Gilead Baptist Church.

The Hannas attended Gilead for special occasions, and a summer revival in Kentucky was a special occasion. As was their custom, the Hannas invited the visiting evangelist for a Sunday meal.

Price and Frances Hanna stood at opposite ends of the long table. Between them were all the children, Brother Mitchell, and more food than you could imagine. "Would you lead our blessing, Brother Mitchell?" Price Hanna said.

Brother Mitchell concluded with an amen. The Hanna family, in unison, said, "amen," and they all sat down to eat.

What a meal it was: chicken, hot biscuits, gravy, big juicy tomatoes, hot buttered corn, and field peas. And that was just on one side of the table. There were also okra, string beans, and a big bowl of blackberry cobbler sitting right in the middle of the table.

The dishes were passed, left to right, and each person took a helping. The cobbler stayed in the middle of the table. As dessert, it would be passed last, after the vegetables had been eaten.

"These are wonderful vegetables, Price," said Brother Mitchell, speaking to Ross's father.

"Thank you," Mr. Hanna replied. "They come from our garden out back."

"How do you have time to work a garden?" Mr. Mitchell continued. "You've certainly got your hands full around here with the other farm work."

"Ross has been a big help with that," Mrs. Hanna said. "He's fifteen now and knows a lot about agriculture."

Brother Mitchell looked at Ross seated across the table. "Ross, would you mind showing me the garden after lunch?"

Ross and Brother Mitchell walked slowly along the small fence that surrounded the garden. Ross leaned down and plucked a large ripe tomato from the vine. "Once tomatoes get ripe you must pick them quickly," he told Brother Mitchell. "If you let them stay too long, they will rot."

The two walked on past the tomatoes, past the beans, and beside the tall stalks of corn. "I'm pleased you have been in the revival each night," said Brother Mitchell. "I know from what your parents say about you that you are serious about church."

Ross and Brother Mitchell took a few more steps. "Yes," said Ross, kicking the dirt with his feet. "I have always been serious about church. My parents have been Christians for as long as I can remember. I've gone to church for as long as I can remember."

"Do you know what becoming a Christian means?" said Brother Mitchell. "Yes, I think I do," said Ross.

"Would you like to become a Christian and follow Christ?"

Ross looked out over the garden, past the fence, into the pasture on the other side.

"Yes, I would," he replied.

Later that day, while working alone in the garden, Ross Hanna gave his heart and life to Jesus. That evening he walked down the aisle at the Gilead Baptist Church and made his decision public. The following Sunday, a warm and beautiful day, he was baptized in the Nolin River which flowed by the church.

Feeling God's Call

At night I would go out in front of the house. I would sit under the maple trees, look up at the sky, and talk to God. I just couldn't see how He could use me because we were poor, and I was crippled.

The glow of the kerosene lanterns spilled through the windows and into the dark night. The light did not reach Ross who was sitting in the front yard under a large maple tree. The lantern light made the house look warm. "It is a warm place," he thought. "Not warm like a favorite blanket on a winter night but warm with parents, brothers, and sisters who love you."

He leaned back and looked up between the limbs of the maple tree. Stars covered the sky. "How far beyond the stars is God?" he wondered. "Ten miles, ten million miles, ten billion light-years?" Then he laughed. "God may be up there," he thought, "but God is also here because I talk to Him all the time." With his eyes open, Ross began to pray.

"I know, God, that You have something You want me to do, but for the life of me I can't figure it out. Right now I don't feel called to anything special. But maybe You'll clear my mind up on that soon, huh, Lord?"

Ross pulled his left knee up under his chin and wrapped his arms around his leg. "I've thought about it, Lord," Ross continued. "I've thought of being an agricultural missionary to China. That sounds like it would be interesting, don't You agree?" Ross paused, waiting for the answer that did not come.

"I know that I'm not cut out to be a preacher. I told the congregation I was called into special service. That didn't mean I wanted to be a preacher. I really don't enjoy that."

Ross stretched his left leg out and leaned back against the tree trunk. "I tell You one thing I've enjoyed," he continued. "I've enjoyed working with the kids from the Glen Dale Baptist Children's Home. It's not far from the church, and on Sundays I teach a Junior girl's Sunday School class and an Intermediate Training Union group.

"Most of these kids have no parents or relatives to look after them. They need someone to love them and teach them. I'm not able to do much. But I love doing what I can.

"And the good thing about it is this. I've been able to get those two groups to help with work in the black community. Some of these people are really hurting, too. Oh, I don't mean they have a broken leg or anything, like I do. I mean they are hurting inside because other people have not been nice to them. Sometimes that can be the worst kind of hurt."

Ross stopped talking. His thoughts drifted back to a year ago when he had met the old, blind, black man walking home from school. Ross grew to love the old man, and the old man loved him. He invited Ross to the black church, and Ross went. He also invited Ross home for Sunday meals.

Ross learned to love the black people he had known so little about. He was embarrassed because many people in his community still thought the color of a person's skin made a difference. "Of course, it doesn't," Ross said to himself. "If only people knew that."

Ross shook himself back into the present and looked up into the sky. "Maybe my special call is to people like this. Maybe I'm to work with the forgotten and neglected people of this world. Is this where You are leading me, Lord?"

The front door slammed. "Who are you talking to, Ross?" his mother called out.

"Oh, no one in particular," he replied.

"Well, come on in. It's time to get to sleep. We've got a lot of work to do tomorrow."

Between my first and second years of college I worked in the Appalachian Mountains around Grayson, Kentucky. I led Vacation Bible Schools and held tent revivals. Later I transferred to Morehead State University so I could work with those forgotten mountain people.

The summer began with meetings in Crane Creek Hollow.

"Hollow. That's a funny word," Ross said to himself as he and two others struggled with the tent pole. "A hollow is where two mountains come together and form a very narrow valley. I wonder how many people know that?" he asked himself.

He would be in this hollow for two weeks. Each day the schedule would be the same: drive the bus and pick up the children, teach Bible school, take the children home, eat lunch, go visiting, eat supper, drive the bus and pick up people for the revival, lead the singing, preach, drive the people home, and fall into bed, exhausted.

Ross looked at his watch. It was five o'clock. The sun was going down, but it was still very hot. The three men perspired heavily as they tugged at the tent ropes.

Suddenly, all three men looked up. An old pickup truck was bouncing up the narrow road that ran beside the clearing. Though the evening sun reflected off the windshield, Ross could tell that the truck was driven by a young girl. As the truck passed, the sun's rays filled the cab. Ross saw a flash of gold.

"Who was that blonde?" Ross asked.

"I couldn't see," said Buster Felty. "The sun was in my eyes. Was she the one driving?"

"No," said Ross returning to his work with the tent. "She was on the passenger's side."

"I couldn't see either," said the other man as he tugged again at the ropes. "But if she was blonde, then it had to be

Betty Jane O'Bryan. She is the only blonde in Crane Creek Hollow."

Ross tied a square knot in the tent rope and stood up straight. "Has she been to the revival yet?"

"I haven't seen her," replied Buster. "I don't think she's been here."

Late that night, after the revival, Ross thought about the girl in the truck. "I only saw her for an instant," he said to himself. "She probably isn't as pretty as I thought. Even so, I think I'll visit her tomorrow and invite her to the revival."

What Do You Say to a Preacher?

The week was half over before my aunt, who was the same age as me, and I went to the revival. Ross was there, singing and preaching in a pair of white pants and a white shirt. We laughed because he looked like an ice-cream man.

The service had begun when Betty Jane and her aunt arrived. They parked the car near the side of the tent and entered from the back.

Ross Hanna was up front behind a small wooden stand. He had on a white shirt and white pants. In his left hand was a hymnal. His right hand moved down, left, right, up, down, left, right, up—keeping time for the hymn. Just to the right of Ross a young girl played an old pump organ. Music filled the tent as her fingers stabbed at the keys, and her legs pumped furiously.

Rain threatened, and the air was sticky and muggy. Even before Ross began his sermon, he was covered with perspiration.

Betty Jane listened intently to what the young preacher said. She was seventeen years old, but she seldom went to church. Her parents were loving, strict, and moral, but they were not Christians.

Betty Jane's grandmother was the only Christian in her immediate family. Betty Jane loved her dearly. Grandmother lived just up the road from Betty Jane's house. On late summer afternoons Grandmother would stand out in her yard and call, "Betty J-a-a-a-a-ne," holding her middle name for what seemed an eternity. "Go call the c-o-o-o-o-o-ws."

Betty Jane knew what to do. She crossed the road, jumped over the barbed-wire fence and went after the cows.

It often meant walking a mile or two, but she always found the cows. All she had to do was get one started toward the barn, and all the others followed.

"They know where to go," she often thought. "They just make me come out here and give them a shove."

When the cows were in the barn, Grandmother would give Betty Jane the keys to the little store her grandfather ran, another hundred yards up the hollow.

"Go get yourself a couple of candy bars," she would say. "You did a good job today."

Betty Jane's grandmother had taken her to church several times. But she had never been to a revival in a tent. And she had never seen a preacher work as hard as this Ross Hanna.

When the service ended, people began filing out of the tent. "I'm going out the back and shake this man's hand," Betty Jane's aunt said. "How about you?"

Betty Jane looked horrified. "No way," she said, "I don't want to shake hands with that guy."

Betty Jane turned, walked through a crowd of people and between several rows of chairs. At the side of the tent, she lifted the flap and ducked under. Safely outside, she walked quickly to the car.

At the back of the tent Ross Hanna's smile turned to a frown. "She was coming my way," he thought. "I was going

to meet her. Then poof, like magic, she's gone." Ross shook a few more hands. Then he excused himself and walked quickly to the side of the tent.

Betty Jane saw him coming, but she had nowhere to go. She felt trapped and nervous. "What do you say to a preacher who dresses like an ice-cream man?" she asked herself.

Ross greeted Betty Jane and tried to hide the nervousness he felt inside. Then he asked if he could take Betty Jane home that evening. She said no.

The next night he asked again. Again she said no.

The third night he asked again. This time she said yes. From then until the end of summer, Ross and Betty Jane spent every Wednesday, Saturday, and Sunday evening together.

> Even as a non-Christian, she was the sweetest girl I had ever met. I was scared to death I was going to fall in love with her.

Every date centered around a church or revival meeting. There was little else to do: no concerts to hear, no baseball games to see, and it certainly would have been improper for a preacher to go to a movie.

Ross looked forward to his dates with Betty Jane. She was beautiful. She was considerate. She was kind. She was gentle. She was fun to be around. Only one thing bothered Ross: Betty Jane was not a Christian.

All summer long Ross talked with Betty Jane about become a Christian. But she almost never talked back. "It's like talking to a blank wall," Ross said to himself. "For seven weeks I've been talking myself blue in the face, and she just ignores me. I wish she would argue with me. That way I would at least know she was listening."

"Ross, get that sour look off your face," Betty Jane said, though not out loud. "I've been listening. I'm just thinking about it, that's all. I don't like to talk and think at the same time. Too many people do that. It gets you into trouble.

"I know I should become a Christian. I grew up in the country, and I have always felt very close to nature and to God. The reason I am not a Christian is because no one ever talked to me about it. So now you're talking to me about it. But hey, back off a little and give me time to think."

Betty Jane took the rest of the summer to think. During the last service that Ross preached before returning to college she walked forward. "I want to give my heart to Christ," she said, standing in front of the pulpit.

Ross smiled and fought to hold back the tears.

Marriage and Seminary

At 3:00 PM on June 3, 1951, we were married at Barrett's Creek Baptist Church. I served as pastor of this church during my last two years of college. In July of 1952, I graduated from Moorehead State University with a degree in elementary education.

During the 1952 school year Ross taught first through fourth grades in a small two-room school and was pastor of three small churches: Barrett's Creek, Wolfe Creek, and Crane Creek, a mission he had begun. He was able to pastor three churches because they had services at different times.

In the fall of 1953, Ross and Betty Jane moved to Louisville, Kentucky, where Ross attended Southern Baptist Theological Seminary. They arrived with $39 and a great desire to learn. Ross resigned as pastor of two churches. He remained as pastor of Crane Creek. This gave him time to study.

To help earn money for expenses, Betty Jane worked in the seminary cafeteria. At night she took classes in child development. What she learned was put to use when their

first child, Stephen Ross, was born during their second year at seminary.

Ross Hanna stayed busy as father, husband, pastor, and student. There were sermons to prepare, Greek and Hebrew lessons to learn, and, of course, Stephen needed attention. At age six weeks, Steven Ross had his first asthma attack. Ross and Betty Jane spent many hours taking Stephen to the doctor and treating his asthma at home.

The schedule at seminary was exhausting, but the learning was exhilarating. Ross and Betty Jane fell asleep each night bone tired but happy. During the second year of seminary Ross began to wonder where he would serve when he graduated.

I heard a speaker in chapel say, "You think you ought to have a call to go as a missionary? What does the Great Commission say? Matthew 28:19 says, 'Go ye therefore, and teach all nations, baptizing them in the name of the Father, and of the Son, and of the Holy Ghost.'"

Ross's brain snapped back to full attention. "This man must be talking directly to me," he thought.

"Nowhere does the Great Commission have anything to say about a call. The Great Commission says that the first command of the Lord is to go," the speaker emphasized. "If you don't get a call to stay, then the Lord says go!"

The speech was short, but Ross remembered the message for a long time. Over and over he thought about what he had heard. Does this mean that everyone is a missionary? Does this mean that I need to go unless I feel God is telling me to stay? If I am to go, where will I serve?

The answer came quickly. Ross heard the president of the Bacone Baptist Indian College in Oklahoma speak in a chapel service. The president talked about his work with the Indians. He talked about how the Indians had been mistreated for so many years. As Ross listened he thought of the people he had worked with: the mountain people of Kentucky and the people in the black community.

Dr. Courts Redford, from the Home Mission Board, scheduled meetings with students interested in the work. Ross talked over his idea with Betty Jane and then met with Dr. Redford.

"I know something about how these people feel," Ross said to Dr. Redford. "I know something about their problems and their hurts. I think I can help them. I think that God may be calling me to work with the Indians."

"If you really think this is where God is leading you," said Dr. Redford, "I want you to write Bailey Sewell. He is head of Indian work for the state of Oklahoma. He may be able to help you."

A Visit to Falls Creek Indian Camp

The Lord will open doors of service to you. If one door closes, another will open. As He shows you opportunities, take them. He will guide you along as you go.

Ross could see the long envelope through the glass of his post office box. He knew the letter was from Bailey Sewell. Quickly he turned the combination knob: 26 right; 32 left; 38 right. The box popped open, and he removed the letter.

Dear Mr. Hanna:

Thank you for your recent letter asking about the possibility of doing Indian mission work in Oklahoma. It seems that your experience would qualify you for this type of work.

I want to invite you to attend the Falls Creek Indian Camp in Davis, Oklahoma, this summer. During this time you can meet me and others involved in the work here and get a feel for what is going on. This firsthand look at the work might help you decide if this is what you really feel God is leading you to do.

If you decide to come, I would like for you to teach a class on prayer to one of our groups. This would let you get acquainted with some of the Indians who attend the camp.

Please let me know of your plans.

Falls Creek Indian Camp is in the rolling hills of the Arbuckle Mountain range, in south central Oklahoma. When Ross and Betty Jane drove through the camp gates, they had little idea what to expect. What they found was entirely to their liking.

The camp was plain. Campers and teachers slept in wooden dormitories. Classes were held under ramadas— shelters with tin roofs, dirt floors, wooden benches, and open sides. In these ramadas, which were spread throughout the campground, classes of fifteen to twenty people met each day to study the Bible and to pray.

On the first morning, the camp came alive just after breakfast. Hundreds of Indians left the main dining hall and walked to their 8:30 classes. Ross and Betty Jane watched as the groups marched single file up and around the small hills of the camp.

"How many Indians tribes are here?" asked Betty Jane.

Ross pulled a piece of paper from his pocket. "Bailey told me, and I wrote it down," he said. "Oh, here it is: Choctaw, Chickasaw, Creek, Cherokee, Kiowa, Seminole, Seneca, Eastern Shawnee, Pawnee, Wyandot, and Quapaw."

The week flew by for Ross and Betty Jane. Ross was either teaching a class or preparing for it, or the two were attending classes themselves or meeting missionaries or talking late into the night with Indian pastors. But the week was inspiring. They met many people, learned many things, and made many Christian friends.

As Ross and Betty Jane walked up the winding dirt trail to the ramada, Ross felt sad. "This is the last morning of camp," he said. "I'm going to miss all our new friends when we go back to seminary.

"But," he continued, "I have felt so at home among these people and have enjoyed this week so much that I think God may be telling me that here is where we should work. I think . . .

He stopped in mid sentence and looked at his watch. "It's only 8:15," he said, "but look."

Twenty yards ahead, under the ramada, his class huddled on their knees in prayer. The people were speaking in an Indian language, and Ross could not understand it.

"The class does not start until 8:30," said Ross, "but everyone's here early. And what are they praying about?"

Ross and Betty Jane walked up to the group. They were met by one of the class members, an Indian who had been to the camp many times before.

"Why is everyone here early, John?" Ross asked. "And what were they praying about?"

"Oh, they've been here for more than an hour," said John. "They came early because of you, and they were praying for you."

"What do you mean they were praying for me?"

"We have known all week why you were here," said John. "We knew that you were thinking about coming here to work with the Indians."

"How did you know that?" Ross asked.

"Oh, word just got around," said John with a smile. "This week these people have gotten to know you. They like you and think you would work well with the Indians. This morning has been a special prayer meeting. This class prayed that you would feel called by God to come and work with the Indians in Oklahoma."

The lump in Ross's throat was so big he could hardly speak. Even as he taught the class, his mind kept flashing back to the sight of the Indians on their knees, praying for

him. When class was over and he had said good-bye to all his friends, he stayed under the ramada to think and pray. Later that day he went to see Bailey Sewell.

"When I saw the Indians kneeling together, praying for me, I saw that as a confirmation of God's call," Ross said. "I want to work out here with the Indians. If you've got a place for me, I'm coming."

An Invitation to Oklahoma

When we got back to seminary, Bailey Sewell called. He said he wanted us to come back to Oklahoma and visit the Spring River Indian Baptist Church on the Quapaw Indian Reservation. I told him we could leave on Friday, after my last class.

Just after 5:00 PM on Friday, Ross and Betty Jane left Louisville. They had a picnic basket filled with sandwiches in the front seat and three relatives in the back seat. The relatives would be relief drivers on the long trip.

During the night, they made their way through Kentucky, Tennessee, and into Arkansas. With occasional stops for gasoline and breaks, they arrived at Spring River at dusk on Saturday.

On Sunday morning Ross was rested and ready to preach at Spring River Baptist. The small church was built of native sandstone. It had one room with a hardwood floor, a tall ceiling, and beautiful oak pews. It sat proudly on the banks of the Spring River, far away from houses or other buildings.

"The church is basically dead now," Ross had been told. "Not many people attend. The area around Spring River was once rich in lead and zinc. Now the mines have played out, and many of the people have moved away."

Ross and Betty Jane did not know how many would

attend that morning—maybe ten, maybe one hundred, maybe none. By the time the service started, twelve were there, including the five who came from Louisville. Ross was not discouraged. He had preached to smaller crowds. And he knew that, given time, he could bring the church back to life.

New Life for Spring River

On December 6, 1956, I was appointed by the Home Mission Board as missionary to American Indians. I graduated from seminary on January 17, 1957, and we went straight to Oklahoma.

The Spring River Indian Baptist Church did come back to life, but it took many months of hard work. First, Ross and Betty Jane had to win the confidence of the Indians. They did this by showing the people that they really cared for them.

When someone was sick, Ross and Betty Jane visited them. When families needed food, the missionaries found a way to provide it. They quickly got involved in most of the problems the Indians faced. The Indians soon responded.

Sunday crowds at church grew from 12 to 19 to 30, then to 56, then higher. Within a year the little church was packed on Sunday mornings. Sunday School attendance was between 80 and 125. The church built an educational building to take care of all the people. Each year Ross baptized twenty-five to fifty new believers. Things couldn't have been better.

Then the bottom dropped out. The US Government offered job training for Indians in the cities. In one year the church's membership dropped to just one family.

It was a blow to Ross and Betty Jane. Now they had to

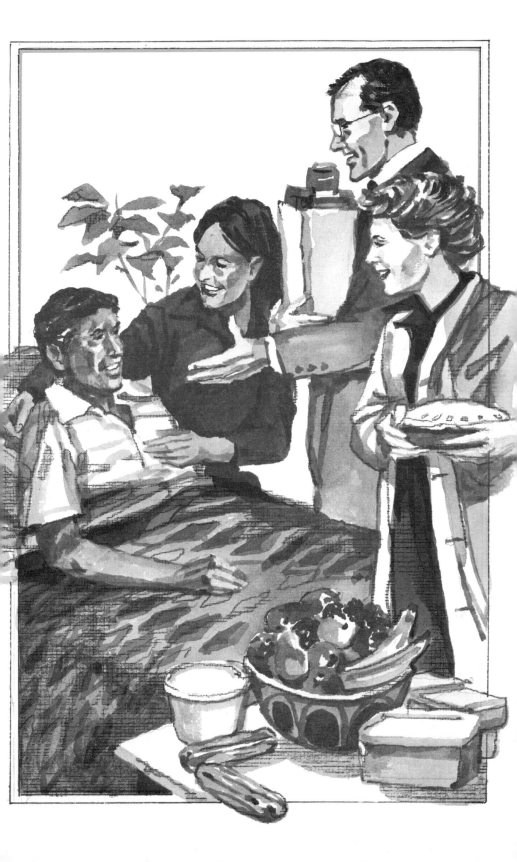

start from scratch again. But Ross remembered what he had told his father at the hospital. "Bad times are a part of life. We must make the best of them and keep on going."

They did keep going. Soon the church was again filled with people. As the congregation grew, Ross trained Indians for leadership positions in the church. They started new programs. Woman's Missionary Union and Brotherhood were begun to help in missions work; GA and RA and Sunbeam organizations were a part of these. Choir and Church Training were also a part of Spring River Baptist Church. The church even gave 25 percent of its money to support the Cooperative Program, Southern Baptists' plan of giving.

For his work at Spring River, Oklahoma Baptists in 1959 gave Ross the "Rural Pastor of the Year Award." It was the first time a pastor of an Indian church had received the award.

> After I became a missionary to the Indians I had the opportunity to speak at World Missions Conferences. These are meetings where missionaries tell others about their work. I've always enjoyed teaching. I hope I do it well.

Ross had just finished speaking about his work with the Indians in Oklahoma. Tama, the Hannas' second child, slept soundly on the front row as people in the crowded auditorium began asking questions. From the third row a hand went up. "Yes," said Ross, nodding.

The man stood. "Did you have any big problems when you went to work with the Indians? I mean, you know, it's a different culture, and they have some strange ways."

Ross stepped from behind the podium and away from the microphone as he spoke. "Oh, I guess we're had a few problems," he said. "But I've worked in the mountains of Kentucky. And the mountain people had some strange ways too. At least they were strange to me at first.

"But whatever their ways," Ross continued, "you still win them to the Lord in the same way. You love them, respect them, try to understand them, and share the gospel with them. When they know you care about them, they will listen to what you have to say."

A woman sitting in the row behind Tama raised her hand. "It tires me out to listen to you talk about your schedule," she said. "Don't you get tired? Doesn't your enthusiasm leave you sometimes?"

Ross laughed. "Oh, do I get tired!" he said, and laughed again. "But I enjoy my work, I always have. I may be exhausted when I go to bed at night, but I'm happy. And that's what counts."

Ross looked out over the crowded auditorium. A hand went up about midway back. Ross pointed to a young man and said, "Yes, what is your question?"

The man slowly stood. "What's the biggest problem you have in winning the Indians to Christ?" the young man asked.

Ross took a deep breath. "The biggest problem we faced when we arrived was the Peyote church."

The young man stood again. "I don't understand," he said "What is a Peyote church?"

"Peyote is a cactus," said Ross. "People smoke or chew the drug that comes from part of the plant. When they do this, they see things that aren't real; it affects them something like a dream."

"But how do they use cactus in a church service?" the young man asked.

"The Peyote service begins around eight at night," Ross said. "Men gather in an adobe building around a mound shaped like a half-moon. During the service they smoke or chew the peyote until they pass out.

"When they wake up they tell everyone what they saw while they were under the influence of the drug. One may say he talked to his mother or father, who told him to do this or that. Another may say he talked to God. This goes on all night. At sunrise they eat breakfast cooked by the women. Then the men go home and sleep all day.

"Some Christian beliefs get mixed up in peyote services," said Ross. Sometimes they use the Bible or someone preaches a sermon. They say they believe in Jesus."

The young woman on the second row raised her hand again. "It seems like a hopeless situation," she said.

"Oh no," said Ross, "it's not hopeless at all. It just takes time to show them that Jesus is the way, not peyote. There is a little story I heard a long time ago that gives me hope," Ross continued. "I'll close by telling it.

"North of Shawnee, Oklahoma, some Indians started a Baptist church on the reservation—the land assigned to them by the US Government. The church did not have a name, and the Indians were trying to decide what to call it.

"One day the offering had been taken, and the Indian pastor was preaching. At the end of the service the chief of the village came down and gave his heart to Jesus. He put one of the offering baskets on the floor and stepped into it.

"'I am giving myself to Jesus,' the chief said, 'because Jesus is the only Way. Indians have lots of religions but there is only one Way. Let's call this the Only Way Baptist Church.'"

"If we work long enough and hard enough," said Ross, "we can show these people the only Way."

Four Years in Santa Fe

Steve's asthma attacks got steadily worse. The doctor said he should move farther west where the air was dryer. He wanted us to go to Albuquerque, New Mexico, or close by, so Steve could take treatments at the Lovelace Clinic, a hospital that specializes in breathing problems.

Ross contacted Dr. Courts Redford at the Home Mission Board about a transfer. Dr. Redford told him a position was

open in Santa Fe, New Mexico, sixty miles from Albuquerque. The Hannas could transfer as soon as they were able. Betty Jane and Steve went immediately. Ross and Tama stayed in Quapaw for six weeks to finish the summer programs.

For the next four years the Hannas lived in Santa Fe. Ross worked as missionary to Indians in the city. He served as chaplain to students at the American Institute of Indian Arts where more than 300 students from 120 Indian tribes studied.

While in Santa Fe, Ross and Betty Jane wrestled with a family problem. Since their marriage, nine years earlier, they had wanted four children. But Betty Jane had difficulty during the births of Steven and Tama. The doctor advised her not to have more children. The answer, they decided, was to adopt.

Because of their love for Indians, Ross and Betty Jane decided to adopt an Indian baby. After being interviewed by the adoption agency, they were told that six babies were available.

When Ross and Betty Jane saw the first baby they had no trouble deciding. "This is the one we want," they both said. "We don't need to see any others."

They named him Kee Chee (a Navajo phrase meaning "red boy"). As the third child in the Hanna family, he brought them all great joy.

To Papago Land

In 1965 we were called to be missionaries for the Papago Indian Reservation. Their tribal headquarters was in Sells, Arizona, near Tucson.

During the long drive to Arizona the children kept their

faces pressed against the car windows. Steve, 11; Tama, 7; and Kee, 4, played the games many children play while riding long distances. They counted cars, cows, oil wells, copper mines, and cowboys.

They looked for familiar faces in the clouds. They imagined strange shapes in the beautiful rock formations that dotted the desert floor. They guessed at the height of the tall cacti as they passed through the Saguaro National Forest near Tucson. They imagined what it would be like to travel through the desert in a wagon train a hundred years ago.

While the children played games in the back seat, Ross tried to remember all he had learned about Indians in Arizona, especially the Papago. In his mind he went down the list he had earlier put on paper.

• More American Indians live in Arizona than in any other state.

• Arizona has more than ninety thousand Indians from fourteen tribes living on nineteen reservations.

• The tribal headquarters of the Papago Indians is in Sells, Arizona. Sells is sixty miles southwest of Tucson and only twenty-five miles north of the Mexican border.

• The Papago reservation is the second largest reservation in the United States. It contains three million acres.

• There are 120 small villages on the reservation but only one Baptist church.

• There is only one paved road running through the reservation.

• To reach some villages by dirt road takes two or three days.

• The dry, harsh climate on the Papago reservation makes farming difficult.

• The Papago may be America's poorest people. Their median family income is about 6 percent of that of an Anglo (white) family.

Ross let out a deep sigh. "What is it?" Betty Jane asked.

Ross mumbled, "I was just thinking that working with

the Papago is going to be a real challenge."

As soon as they arrived in Sells, Ross discovered the challenge was bigger than he had imagined. "You can come and work with us if you want, but we are not changing," the Indians quickly told Ross and Betty Jane. "We've been in the same spot, on the same land, for ten thousand years. We will be here long after you're gone. You can try to teach us about your religion, but we won't accept it. When you leave, everything will be as it was before you came."

But Ross Hanna had a response for the Indians. This is what he told them.

"I'm going to love you. I'm going to show you I love you by how I act. You will want to know why I love you, and then you will be curious about Jesus who loves all of us.

"When you're in the hospital, I will visit you. When you're hungry, I'll find something to eat. When you lose your wife or child, I will be there with you. In good or bad times I will be there to help you and be your friend.

"You need to hear what I have to say about Jesus. You will not listen to me now, but before too long you will want to hear what I have to say."

We talked to the Papago judge. She told us about the neglected children on the reservation who had nowhere to go. She told us about a two-year-old girl who was found under a bridge, almost dead. I asked if Betty Jane and I could keep her.

Betty Jane held the baby bottle to the little girl's mouth and squinted her eyes to hold back a tear. "Drink this," she said. "It will help you get strong again."

The girl lay motionless. She was cute, but thin. Very thin. Her eyes were hollow and stared blankly out the window beside the small wooden crib.

Ross reached down and held the little girl's hand. Her thin arm was covered with mosquito and flea bites. "No telling how long she lived under that bridge," he said. "This kind of thing makes me sad and angry. How could

anyone let this happen to a little child? God must be very sad when He sees this happen."

Betty Jane held the bottle at the child's mouth, but the little girl still did not drink.

"How long can we keep her at our house?" Betty Jane said to Ross.

"The judge has given us custody of the child for the time being," he replied. "The judge said we could keep her until she gets well—if she gets well," he added. "After that the judge will find a foster home for her."

"Let's keep her here in our room," said Betty Jane. "That way we can be close by if anything happens during the night."

She turned from the crib, put her arms around Ross and hugged him tightly. "I want this little girl to live," she said, tears streaming down her face. "I want her to have a chance in life. I want her to have someone to love her. I want her to love someone. I want her to grow up, play games, climb trees, have friends."

Betty Jane nursed the baby back to health. Slowly, she regained her strength. But it took almost three years before the baby was healthy enough to be placed in a foster home.

In September, 1967 another baby entered the Hanna household. She was Wesa Lin Hanna, born to Ross and Betty Jane and given a Cherokee name meaning "Cat." Wesa and the other Hanna children had plenty of play-mates. More Indian children had come to live with the Hannas. Some were children of alcoholics. Some were children of parents who were in jail. Some had been abandoned by their parents. Some were children of parents killed in automobile accidents.

Soon the Hannas' small house was overflowing. "This reminds me of the Mother Goose story about the woman who lived in a shoe," said Ross. "She had so many children she didn't know what to do. Well," he looked at Betty Jane and smiled, "what are we going to do?"

They began by putting beds in the Sunday School class rooms, but the Hannas needed help to take care of the children. Doris Christensen, a worker who came with them from New Mexico, helped. So did summer missionaries sent by the Home Mission Board, missions volunteers, and local church members. A retired school superintendent even gave the Hannas a trailer to use for bedrooms. The Hannas and the volunteers were able to take care of ninety-five homeless children.

Soon, word got around the reservation. "The Hannas care for our children," the Indians were saying. Gifts of money came in. Some came from the Indians, some from churches who had heard about the Hannas' work. In three years and eight months the Hannas built a children's home near the church. "Now neglected children will have some-where to go," Ross said, "even after we are gone."

The Hannas began a kindergarten for four-year-olds. The next year they extended it to five-year-olds. The third year they began a day-care center for children whose parents worked. As the work with children grew, so did the relationship between the Hannas and the Papago adults.

"Hi, I'm Ross Hanna . . . " and he would get no further. "You're the man who helps our children," the Indians would respond. "Please come in. We will listen to what you have to say now. You have earned the right to be heard."

Popcorn at Friendship Center

In 1970 the Home Mission Board asked us to transfer to Tucson and begin the first Christian Social Ministries program in the state. We were assigned to work at Friendship Baptist Center. The last missionary had left two years ago, and the work was almost dead.

"What do you think?" asked Betty Jane, looking at the front of Friendship Center. Ross looked left and right. The building sat on a corner lot, its red-brick front surrounded by large shrubs. "Plenty of room," he thought. It was about the size of two small houses put together.

The front door opened onto a large room. Ross's heels clicked against the tile as he walked to the center of the room. To the left was a large sliding door used to divide the room for extra classroom space. At the far end of the room a door on the right opened into a smaller room. From that room other doors opened into still smaller rooms. "The building is fine, and it's in a good location, close to the school. I think it's got possibilities," said Ross. "But I need to get one thing before we begin."

Two retired schoolteachers asked what I needed to begin work at the center. They said they would buy it for me. I told them it would cost $350. They said, "Fine. What is it?" I told them I needed a commercial popcorn popper. And you know what? They went out and bought it.

Ross and Betty Jane reached the street with the popcorn just as children were beginning to walk past on the way from school.

"Would you like some popcorn?" Ross asked as the first group of children passed. Within a few minutes children

crowded around Ross and Betty Jane. The bags of popcorn disappeared quickly, and Betty Jane went into the center for more.

"How come you're giving this away?" asked one child, his mouth full of popcorn. Ross looked down at the small boy. He was dressed in faded jeans and his shirt was torn at the side. His feet were bare and very dirty. Ross ran his hand through the boy's uncombed hair. "Because we like you," Ross said.

"Who is we?" the little boy shot back.

"The people here at the Friendship Center," Ross replied.

A little girl dropped her empty sack into the large metal trash can. "Are you going to be out here again?" she asked.

The rest of the children got quiet as they awaited the answer.

"I sure am," said Ross. "Next Tuesday."

A boy's voice came from somewhere near the back: "Can we get some more popcorn then?"

"You sure can," said Ross. "Right after we have Bible stories and activities in the center building. All you've got to do is ask your parents if you can come."

The next Tuesday 150 children came to the center after school. "Where in the world did all these children come from?" asked Betty Jane, not really expecting an answer.

"I really don't know," said Ross. "But let's just thank the Lord for them. The programs are off to a good start."

Finding Other Places of Need

Once we got the work at Friendship Center started, we started looking around Tucson for another needy area. It didn't take long to find one.

Pascua Village was once on the outskirts of Tucson. It was settled by Yaqui Indians, Mexican Indians whose main tribe was on the Yaqui River, many miles south of Tucson. During the Mexican Revolution some of the Yaquis came to the Tucson area and settled outside of town.

But Tucson grew rapidly, and the land where the Indians lived became suburbs, then part of the city itself. Though the city surrounded the area, Pascua Village enjoyed few modern services. When the Hannas first visited the area, there were no paved streets, no city lights, and no city sewer system.

Most people in Pascua Village were unemployed. Drug dealing was common. It was not safe for an outsider to walk the streets, even during the day. Some children went to high school, some didn't. Those who did rarely finished. No one made it to college. It was an area of great need.

Ross drove through Pascua Village with the chairman of the Yaqui Indian tribe. They passed row after row of old homes. Dirty children played in the streets or in vacant lots filled with abandoned cars or household garbage.

"We need help here," said the chairman as he turned into the driveway of an old building. "I want you to begin a center, just like the one you have at Friendship."

"You know I am here to do mission work," Ross said. "What do you want me to do in Pascua Village?"

The chairman smiled and raised his right eyebrow. "I

51

know this is going to sound strange," he said. "But I want you to come here and work for one year without mentioning your religion. I mean no prayer, no Bible study, no religious songs, nothing. If you can do this, you will gain the confidence of my people. You will earn the right to be heard, and you can then say anything about religion you want to."

Ross smiled on the inside. "Earn the right to be heard," he thought. "That's the same thing I heard out on the Papago Reservation. It was true there. It is true here. It is true in most mission situations," he thought. "You do have to gain the respect of people before they will listen to you."

"I will do it," Ross said quickly.

The chairman jerked his head back in mock surprise. "I didn't think you would agree," he said. "At least not so quickly."

"I agree because my programs will sell themselves," Ross said. "During the first year we will hold day camps for children. We will teach adults how to do crafts and how to read. And when the year is over, I will teach them about Jesus.

"Now there's only one small problem left," Ross continued. "Where will the center be located?" The chairman opened the car door and stepped out. "Please follow me," he said.

> The chairman showed me this large, cement block building. The YMCA owned it, but it had not been used in years. We replaced 157 window panes, painted, repaired, swept, and mopped. When the Pascua center was ready, we got another popcorn popper and went to work.

The people responded quickly, as Ross knew they would. Ross kept his promise to the chairman and mentioned nothing religious during center activities. But word soon got around. People in Pascua Village knew the Hannas were Baptist missionaries, and they often asked for special prayer.

One morning the sun was beating down on the newly painted Pascua Center. But the air was dry, and inside the center it was cool. In the front room women worked with ceramics in a craft class. One painted a rooster, another painted a small bowl.

In the next room, ten women and two men sat in a semicircle around a local volunteer who was leading a literacy class. Ross stood at the door. For a few minutes he watched the craft class. Then he watched the literacy class.

"A-E-I-O-U, those are the vowels," said the teacher. "Juanita, can you say them?" The young Mexican woman looked up. Her tiny, shy voice could barely be heard as she struggled for the right sounds.

"Ahh---E---Ahhee---Aw---Ooh."

"That's a good start, Juanita," said the teacher. "Now let's all try it. A-E-I . . . "

Ross was distracted by a noise outside. A woman ran up the gravel driveway beside the center. She was screaming something he could not understand.

The front door of the center flew open. The woman rushed into the room, almost knocking over a craft table near the door. She was about fifty-five years old, short, and a little thin. Her face was dark and smooth, and her black hair was filled with tiny specks of grey. The bracelets on her right arm shook violently as she gestured with her hands and yelled.

"*Su brazo no esta vivo!*" she said as she rushed up to Ross. Ross looked at the woman, trying to understand.

"*Ayudeme! Su brazo no esta vivo!*" she yelled again and clasped her hands together under her chin as if to say please, please. The woman knew that Ross did not understand. She quickly turned her head to the left and right and calling out in Spanish, "*Su brazo esta frio, no esta vivo. Por favor ore por el.*"

One of the women in the craft class rushed over. "What's she saying?," Ross asked. "I don't understand Spanish."

"I do not know what it means," the woman said in

broken English, "but what she says is this: Help me. His arm is cold. It is not living. Please pray for him."

Ross looked at the woman, who was sobbing now, her face buried in her hands. Ross put his hand on her shoulder. "Please calm down," he said, knowing that she did not understand what he was saying. Ross turned back to the other woman. "Please find out what happened and what we can do."

It took fifteen minutes of translation to get the complete story. The woman's son worked at a bottling factory. His arm had been caught in some machinery and had been severed near the shoulder. Doctors at the hospital had sewn the arm back on, but the blood was not flowing into the arm. "*No esta vivo.*" It is not living, the woman kept saying over and over in Spanish.

Through the interpreter, the woman asked Ross to pray that her son's arm would live. "*Por favor ore por el,*" she said, sobbing into her sleeve.

A thousand thoughts rushed through his mind. "I will pray," he thought. "But God may not answer the prayer. Or the answer we get may not be the one this woman wants. How will I handle it if her son loses his arm?"

Ross turned to the interpreter. "Tell her that I will pray for her son. Tell her you will translate the prayer for her."

"Lord, we know You are the Great Physician. We know that You have the power to heal the sick. Today we pray for this young man whose arm was severed in the accident. If it is in Your will, we pray that the man's arm will heal. If not, we pray that You will give the man and his mother the strength and courage they will need to face the problems ahead. In Christ's name. Amen."

At lunch, Ross told Betty Jane what had happened that morning. "You really should go to the hospital and see the man," Betty Jane kept urging.

"I really don't want to," Ross kept saying. "It is not likely that the doctors will be able to save his arm. His mother will think that my prayer did no good. She doesn't understand that you don't get everything you pray for."

"Well," Betty Jane continued, "I think you should go anyway. She may not understand. But at least she will know that you care."

Ross drove slowly, as slowly as he could. The woman had been so emotional this morning. "What will she be like this afternoon?" he asked himself. His mind quickly jumped to the worse thing that could possibly happen. "The young man will lose his arm," he thought. The mother will tell everyone in the village that God did not answer my prayer. She will say that God does not listen to us, and why should others listen to us?

Ross parked and rode the elevator up to the third floor. He rounded the corner and stopped at the nurse's station. "Maybe the man is in intensive care and can't have visitors," he thought. "Room 312," said the young nurse. "Five doors down on the right."

Ross stood before the closed door. His heart beat so loudly he could almost hear it. His hand went up to knock, then froze in midair. The door flew open from the inside, and there was the woman.

Her words came fast. All Ross had time to say was "I'm sorry, *no hablo Espanol* (I don't speak Spanish)."

The woman grabbed his hands and almost yanked him through the door. She said something else in Spanish. Ross could only say *"No hablo Espanol."*

She pulled him to the other side of the large white curtain that separated the two beds in the room. Beside the man's bed stood a nurse holding a plastic tray filled with pill bottles. "Do you understand what she is telling you?" the nurse said to Ross.

"I don't understand a thing," Ross said.

"She is telling you to feel his arm. The one that was severed in the accident."

The woman took Ross's hand and gently placed it on her son's arm. Ross's heart thumped even faster. Ross looked at the man, then up at the nurse.

"The arm is warm, yes?" said the nurse. Ross looked back at the man.

"Yes," he said, then hesitated and smiled broadly. "Yes, it is! Praise the Lord!"

Pascua Village Responds

The story about the man's arm spread throughout the Pascua community. The people soon understood that we cared for them. I could have begun religious services soon after that, but I kept my promise to the chairman.

After a year, Ross began religious activities at the center. "My programs will sell themselves," he had told the chairman with confidence. Now the center was filled with people.

Things happened quickly. The YMCA agreed to sell the Pascua Center building for twenty thousand dollars. The Home Mission Board provided five thousand dollars for the down payment, and the local Baptist association gave money for the monthly payments.

Ross and Betty Jane started Sunday services at the Pascua Center. During the week children attended Bible study along with their other activities. Ross started a medical clinic at the Pascua Center. Later, with the help of a mobile medical clinic, he helped start eight permanent medical centers in needy villages in the Tucson area and in southern Arizona.

Next, Ross focused his attention on the poor living conditions of the Indians in Pascua Village. He helped the Indians get a government grant for portable bathrooms to be built onto each house in the community. Working with the tribal council, he helped convince the city to pave the roads in the village. Soon they had city lights, city sewage

service, and eight-hundred thousand dollars for new houses in Pascua Village.

Pascua was the toughest place we ever worked. I'm glad God prepared us by letting us work in all the other places first. Now we want to see work get started in other areas. There are so many hurting people out there. There is so much to do, and so little time to do it.

Ross turned the blue pickup truck onto Calle Sur, one of the streets near the Pascua Center. Beside Ross sat Cliff Williams, a seminary student who had volunteered to work for Ross for a year. Cliff's thin hair and full beard made him look older than his twenty-five years.

When the truck stopped, Cliff jumped from the cab and opened the tailgate as Ross sounded the horn. Children scampered to the truck from five houses nearby.

Cliff greeted the children and gave each a bag of groceries. Back in the cab, he turned to Ross. "Counting me, you have about fifty volunteers," Cliff said. "Do you think you will be able to relax a little now?"

Ross shook his head. "Not on your life," he quickly replied. "The extra help will allow us to do more. We are just starting our third center in the Manzo area of Tucson. It's a very needy community. I also want us to begin a mission center in every town along the Arizona-Mexican border."

Cliff took a deep breath. "In every town along the border?" he exclaimed. "Are you serious?"

"Very serious," Ross said. "I've already been down along the border talking to some people about getting it started. There's always more to do," he said. "No matter where you go there are hurting people who need help."

Home Is Where the Hurt Is

It's a good life to be a missionary. It's happiness.

After dinner Ross and Betty Jane sat on the swing behind their house. Even though it was summer the night air was dry and cool. The sky was cloudless, and thousands of stars sparkled in the distance.

"We got a new volunteer today," said Ross. "We had a long talk while we were delivering food."

Betty Jane picked up a sweater and put it around her shoulders. "What did you talk about?" she asked.

"Oh, a lot of things," Ross replied. "For one thing, he asked why we did this kind of work and if we ever got tired of it."

"What did you say," Betty Jane asked.

Ross looked over at her with a little grin. "What would you have said?" he asked.

Betty Jane looked up into the sky and thought for a minute. "I'd say that we get tired, but we never get tired of doing our job.

"The Lord has called us to work with the forgotten, the poor, and the hurting in our land. We have always made our home among these people: with the mountain people of Kentucky, the Indians of Oklahoma, and Arizona and the people in the inner city of Tucson.

"I'd say that our work has been fun and exciting because we have been doing something worthwhile, something God wants us to do.

"I'd say we are just common ordinary people who are happy doing what we are doing. And I wouldn't change that for a million dollars."

Ross kept his eyes focused on the stars. "That's exactly what I told him," he said. "That's exactly what I told him."

Important Dates in the Lives of Ross and Betty Jane Hanna

Ross Harmon Hanna born, March 19, 1928

Betty Jane O'Bryan born, February 8, 1932

Ross becomes a Christian, July, 1943

Ross ordained to the ministry, January, 1950

Betty Jane becomes a Christian, July, 1950

Ross and Betty Jane married, June 3, 1951

Ross and Betty Jane appointed as missionaries to the American Indians, December 6, 1956

The Hannas move to Oklahoma, 1957-1961

The Hannas move to New Mexico, 1961-1965

The Hannas move to Arizona, 1965-1970

Remember

• What game was Ross Hanna playing when he had his accident? How long was he in the hospital? Has sickness or an accident kept you in bed or in the hospital for a week or more? What did you think about during that time? How did you feel?

• When Ross came home after his accident, what did his mother teach him to do? What skills have your parents taught you? What do you and your parents enjoy doing together?

• Where was Ross when he became a Christian? What are some of the things that could have led him toward this decision? How could you help one of your friends become a Christian, or how could someone help you?

• Betty Jane's parents were not Christians at first. What difference is there between being good and moral and being a Christian?

• What things in Ross and Betty Jane's life helped them in their work as missionaries? What are you doing now that could help you in your work later?

• Why were the Indians at the Falls Creek Indians Camp praying for Ross? How did God answer their prayers? How has God answered prayer in your life?

• How did the Hannas start work at the Friendship Center in Tucson? If you were given the same challenge how could you have done it?

• What were some of the problems in Pascua Village? How did Ross help to solve the problems? Are there areas in your community or city with the same type of problems? How could you or someone else help?

• Where else would the Hannas like to begin mission centers? What are some of the activities at the mission centers in Tucson? What promise did Ross make to the chairman of Yaqui tribe?

• The Hannas enjoy their work even though it is very difficult. Why?

About the Author

Wayne Grinstead is Associate Director, Communication Division, Home Mission Board. With his wife (Jane), daughter (Jill), and son (Bill) he lives in Decatur, Georgia, six miles from downtown Atlanta.

Wayne is a graduate of the University of Georgia and likes University of Georgia football games. He also pulls for his daughter's gymnastic team, his son's tee-league baseball team, and his wife's piano students. In his spare time he enjoys reading, conducting choral music, running in the Peachtree Road Race, and playing with his home computer.

BROADWAY